POWER
POINT

Cover Art: Ingo and Jane Muschenetz
Cover Design: Ingo Muschenetz
Book Design and Layout: Ingo Muschenetz
All fonts, graphics, artworks, and designs used with permission

ISBN: 9781962405027

Sheila-Na-Gig Editions
Russell, KY
Hayley Mitchell Haugen, Editor
www.sheilanagigblog.com

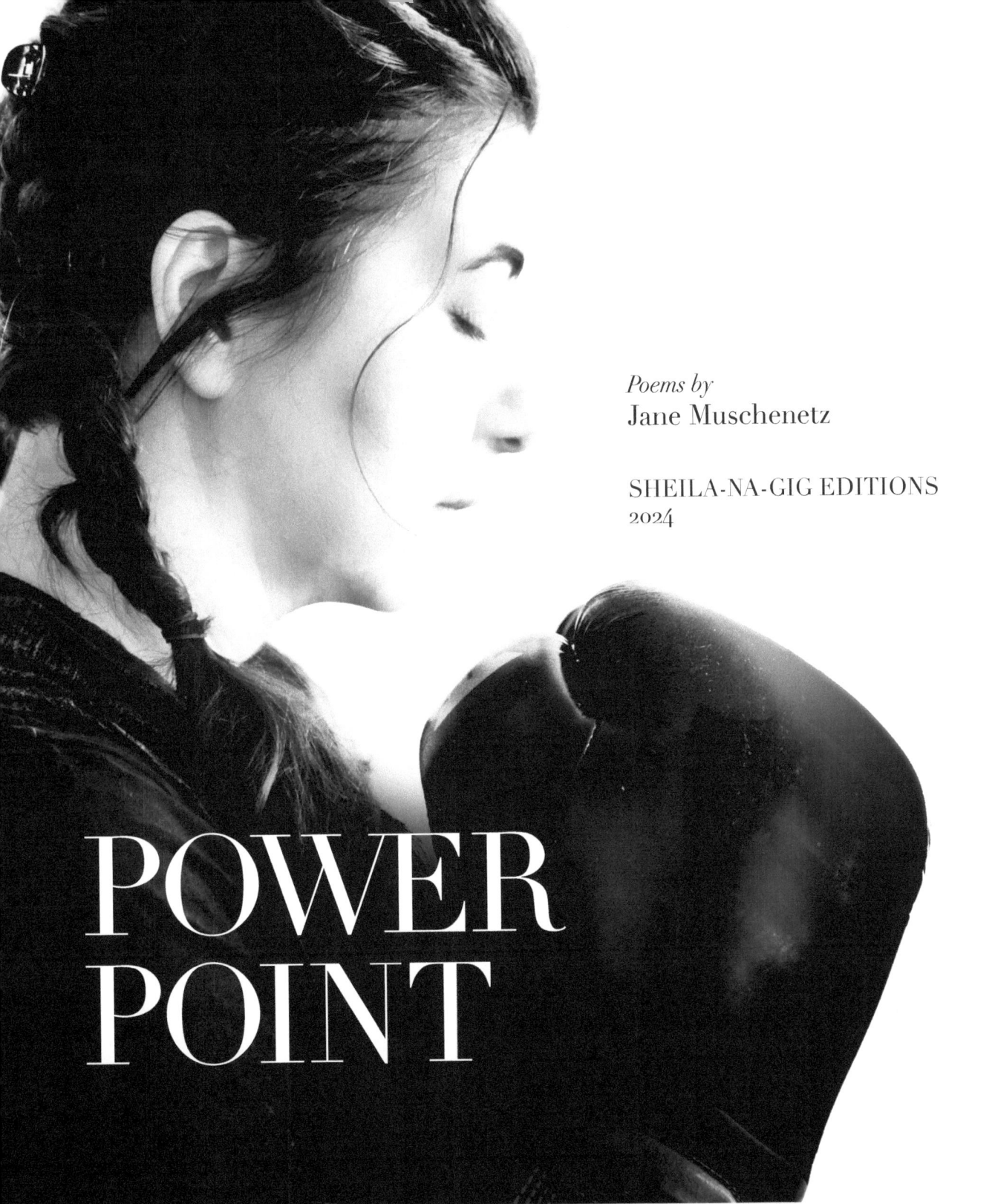

Poems by
Jane Muschenetz

SHEILA-NA-GIG EDITIONS
2024

POWER
POINT

ACKNOWLEDGMENTS

Heartfelt gratitude to the publications that first offered a home to the following poems, some in slightly different variations:

A Plate of Pandemic, "The Earth Remembers Her Teenage Years"

Cathexis North West Press, "You are 600% Hotter Than the Sun," **National Press Women Communications Prize in Creative Verse Recipient, Best of the Net Nominee**

Meat For Tea, "Point of Order, or 'A Progressive Kind of Danger'" and "Failure to Thrive, a Point of Inflection," **Pushcart Prize Nominee**

Rise Up Review, "Breaking Point (Woman. Life. Freedom.)"

San Diego Poetry Annual, "Stop This Poem!"

S/He Speaks, Moonstone Arts Anthology: Volume 2, "She"

Whale Road Review, "100% MOM," **Best of the Net Nominee**

Writers Resist, "Point Blank" and "Gender Neutral," also published in *All the Bad Girls Wear Russian Accents* (Kelsay Books)

Writing in a Woman's Voice, "The Wolves at the Door" and "Inspiration Point," **Charter Oak Prize Semifinalist**

"If the world were only pain and logic, who would want it?"

—Mary Oliver

Author's Note

Too often, women and change-makers are dismissed as "hysterical, emotion-driven, irrational." *Power Point* turns this notion on its head, presenting meticulously researched 'data poems' to make the case for a more compassionate world. By blending traditional and hybrid formats, I aim to expose the status quo as a malleable reality that can and must be questioned, improved, and represented in more ways than one.

Microsoft PowerPoint™ software was used to create several of the 'pointed' poems about 'power' dynamics in this collection.

TABLE OF CONTENTS

[1] A. Chen, "Women Die More from Heart Attacks Than Men Unless ER Doc Is Female," *Scientific American*, 2018; B. Casteel, "Women Don't Get to Hospital Fast Enough During Heart Attack," *American College of Cardiology*, 2015

[2] A. Branigin, "Women 32% More Likely to Die Post-op if Their Surgeon is a Man," *The Washington Post*, Jan. 2022

[3] "Gender inequality and harassment remain a challenge in surgery," *Bulletin of the American College of Surgeons*, Sep. 2019

[4] V. Bolotnyy, N. Emanuel, "How Unpredictable Schedules Widen the Gender Pay Gap," *Harvard Business Review,* July 2022; "National Snapshot: Poverty among Women & Families," *National Women's Law Center,* Dec. 2020

[5] "Providing Unpaid Household and Care Work in the US," *Institute Women's Policy Research*, Brief Paper #C487, Jan 2020; K. Johnson, "At the Office, Unrewarded Work Often Falls to Women," *Boston Globe,* July 2022

[6] "National Snapshot: Poverty Among Women & Families," *National Women's Law Center,* Dec. 2020

[7] L. Chukhno, "Why Women Hold 2/3rd of the Nation's Student Debt," *Earnest,* Nov. 2021

[8] "Maternal Mortality and Maternity Care in the US...," Issue Brief, *The Common Wealth Fund,* Nov. 2020

[9] Senator Hattie Caraway (1932), Justice Sandra Day O-Connor (1981), Senator Carol Moseley Braun (1993), Justice Ketanji Brown Jackson (2022)

[10] T. LeFlouria, "Criminal Justice Reform Won't Work Until It Focuses on Black Women," *Washington Post*, Feb. 2021

POINT OF ORDER, OR 'A PROGRESSIVE KIND OF DANGER'

The fact that you can't give me a straight answer about something as fundamental as 'what a woman is' underscores the dangers of the kind of progressive education . . . we are hearing about.

—Sen. Marsha Blackburn (TN) to Judge Ketanji Brown Jackson,
US Supreme Court Confirmation Hearings, 2022

In North America, *a woman is*
- 2 times more likely than a man to die from a heart attack in an emergency room[1]
- 32% more likely to die post-op if her surgeon is a man[2]
- 70% less likely than a man to be a surgeon[3]
- 20% less paid than a man for the same labor[4]
- fielding 60-75% of unpaid/emotional/social labor at home (child/elder care, housework, meal planning, etc.) and work (committee chairing, volunteering, event management, etc.)[5]

In United States, *a woman is*
- 35% more likely than a man to live in poverty[6]
- holding 2/3 of all student loan debt[7]
- 5 times more likely to die during/after giving birth than in a comparable country[8]
- white
  - her first appointment to the United States Senate happened in 1932[9]
  - her first appointment to the United States Supreme Court happened in 1981[9]

In the case *a woman is*
- black
  - her maternal mortality rate is 3 times as high as a white woman's[8]
  - her pay rate is 20% less[6]
  - her incarceration rate is 2 times more[10]
  - her first appointment to the United States Senate happened in 1993[9]
  - her first appointment to the United States Supreme Court happened in 2022[9]
  - . . .

100% MOM, A POWERPOINT POEM ABOUT WOMEN AND LABOR[11]

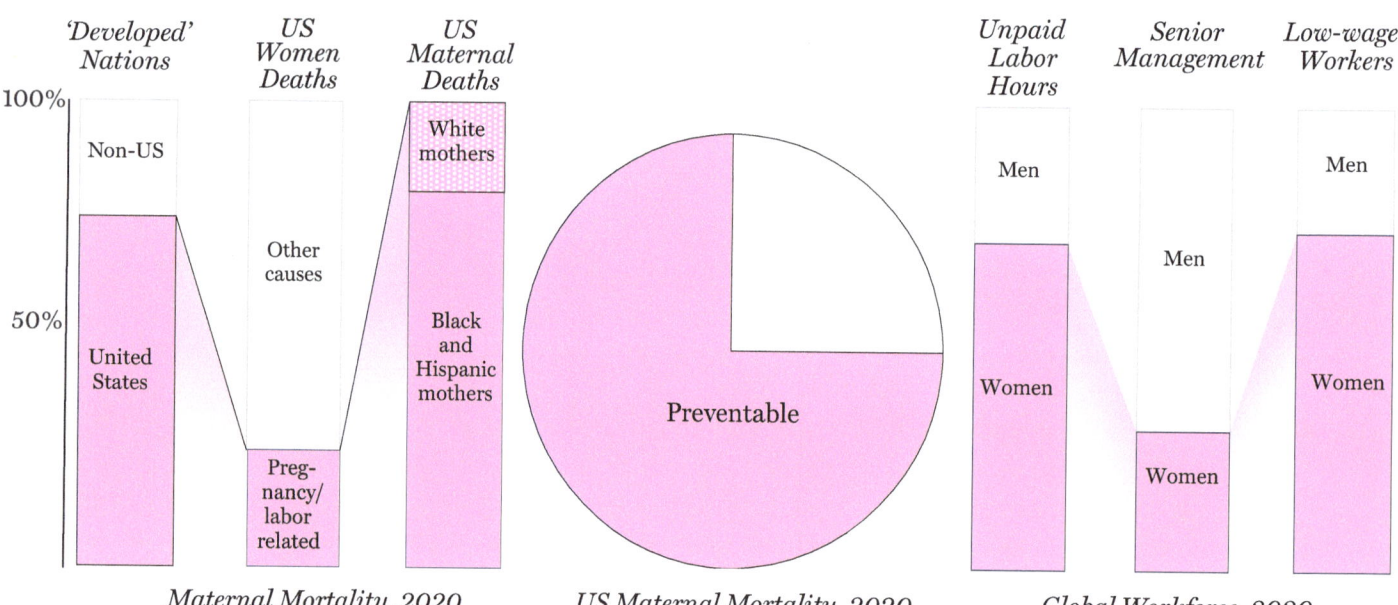

1. Moms are 5 times more likely to die giving birth in the US than moms in other, "equally developed" lands.

2. Some of these moms we can't save, but most, we can.

'Developed' Nations | US Women Deaths | US Maternal Deaths

100%

Non-US

United States

Other causes

Preg-nancy/labor related

White mothers

Black and Hispanic mothers

50%

Maternal Mortality, 2020

Preventable

US Maternal Mortality, 2020

Unpaid Labor Hours | Senior Management | Low-wage Workers

Men

Women

Men

Women

Men

Women

Global Workforce, 2020

3. Black and Hispanic moms die more frequently than do White. We study this, make charts / policies, and write

4. about labor (paid and unpaid), status, values of the hour . . .

5. What is the "real cost" of good? Is knowledge power?

[11] Data sources include: "Life Stages and Populations by Sex," CDC, NCHS; "Most pregnancy-related deaths are preventable," Hear Her Campaign, *CDC*, 2022; "The U.S. Maternal Mortality Crisis Continues to Worsen: An International Comparison," *Commonwealth Fund*, 2022; "The World's Women 2020 Trends and Statistics," *United Nations*; *Oxfam International Inequality Reports*: 2020, 2021, "Hard Work is not Enough: Women in Low-Paid Jobs," *National Women's Law Center*, July 2023; Detailed citation in appendix.

SHE

is the beginning
Mother
Maker
from scant seeds—life
from bare cupboards—dinner
from hard walls—home
Unpaid Labor
pains their father, who
truly believes he works more hours
Necessity, they say
is a mother too
her child is
Invention

THE WOLVES AT THE DOOR

when the doorbell rings, I think like a mother thinks, in little steps
pounding to the entryway, *My Heart,*
inside my body (which is inside the bathtub) ready to leap . . .

she is neither city-folk nor country-wise,
my Zoom-blooded girl, my nightly tucked away treasure—

will she remember to not blindly open the door
like the little goats in the story who outsmarted the wolf? or
will I need to rise, slick and streaming through the house
grab her to safety, like all good mothers, coiled to spring
even the ones taking a quiet bath on the last day of their menstrual cycle and
especially the ones who follow the news cycle?

will she remember to pretend, like I taught her,
that no one is home? or, at least ask who it is at the door,
come back to me
(even though I just told her: Mama is not to be disturbed unless it's an emergency)?

when the doorbell rings, I think like a Jewish (Muslim/Black/Asian/Native Am./Etc . . .)
mother thinks
of all *those* things
I have not yet taught her.

BREAKING POINT (WOMAN. LIFE. FREEDOM.)

for your own good they will tell you:
"It's for your own good," and they will bind your feet
they will beat you to death for not wearing your headscarf
and they won't let you into med school, for your own good

they will rape you in the streets and force you to marry at 13,
and at 9, and at 6 years old, and at no years at all, infant girl
when all you take from this world is a breath, they will take it back
smother you, for your own good, and for your mother's own good too

they will lock you in the house as slave labor
for your own good, they will burn your face with acid,
burn you alive at the stake, at the public bus stop,
cut you off from your friends and your God

for your own good, they will cut your tongue out,
cut your hands off with an axe, cut your clitoris from your body,
cut your access to healthcare and tell you this
is how it is.
 How?!
it has always been
 How?!
it must and should be, for your own good
and for a long time

for a very long time

you will believe them.

MAKE BELIEF

Let us pretend, just for this lifetime, that we are not angels
that we have no wings, no powers beyond the ordinary
to perceive, to dance with universes, that our senses
(being only human) cannot taste possibility and time
as anything but linear and fixed, cannot mix truths
bursting in and out of existence, varied in color,
wavelength, and dimension—infinite, nuanced,
burning with intention, the multifaceted
exponential potential *of all things*,
eludes us! Let us despair and fret
over our impediments and
limitations, as if they
were reality and
mortality—

                    Did you forget already?
                    Did you pretend too well?

A cup of the Sun's core produces ~60 milliwatts of thermal energy. By volume . . . less than that of a human [350 mW]. In a sense, you are hotter than the Sun—there's just not as much of you.

—Henry Reich, *Minute Physics*

YOU ARE 600% HOTTER THAN THE SUN

Speaking roughly, in terms of heat
generated per every human inch, you give
off more milliwatts—surge/energy. Only
the Sun is bigger . . . *it matters.*
We are all blinded
by love, the expanding/contracting
universe is just another metaphor
for longing, and life—its own purpose.
How dazzling, this science!
Consider falling for a physicist—
the painstakingly slow way they undress
mathematical mysteries,
talk about *bodies in motion*
gets me every time—space
—continuum, part, particle—
Atomic. Incandescent! You
are, pound-for-pound, more Life-Source,
more Bomb, more Season-Spinning Searing Center
Heart/Engine/Radiating Nuclear Dynamic
than the Sun. Can't look directly
in the mirror? *Small Wonder!* Imagine—

none of us powerless.

Fig. 1 (⅙th you)

LOW POINT

The rate of US childhood poverty reached its lowest point in 2021 due to the temporary pandemic child tax credit emergency relief program.[12]

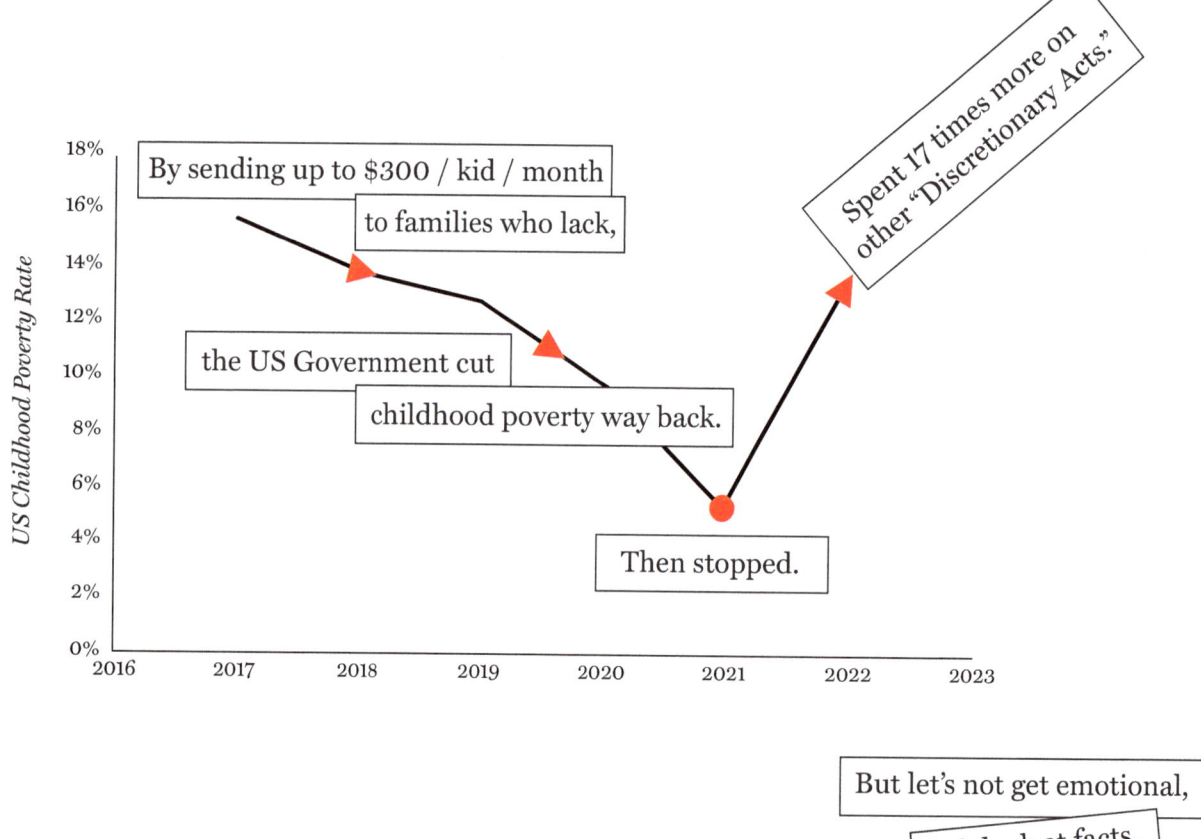

[12] "The SPM child poverty rate more than doubled, from 5.2 to 12.4 percent from 2021 to 2022," Supplemental Poverty Measures, 2017-2022, *US Census*; "The Expanded Child Tax Credit Briefly Slashed Child Poverty," *NPR.org*, 2022. "The Expanded Child Tax Credit Is Gone. The Battle Over It Remains," *NY Times*, 2022. (Congress approved $1.7T in 2022 discretionary spending. The pandemic child tax credit expansion cost was ~$100B per year.) Detailed citation in appendix.

EARNING POINTS

Health was spent on bills,
not the other way around
Time was spent at work
not at (Betsy's?) Christening
Soul and Body we paid
for House and Hearth
and now the taste of new shoes is sour,
our kids aren't grateful (they wanted the other kind instead.)
Wasn't that also what we wanted, another kind
of life? (at least we can afford the therapy, at least this
deep, gnawing hunger is metaphorical)

Threadbare clothes thickened my skin
enough to not take silver-lined spoons for granted,
enough to know a raw deal when I see one.

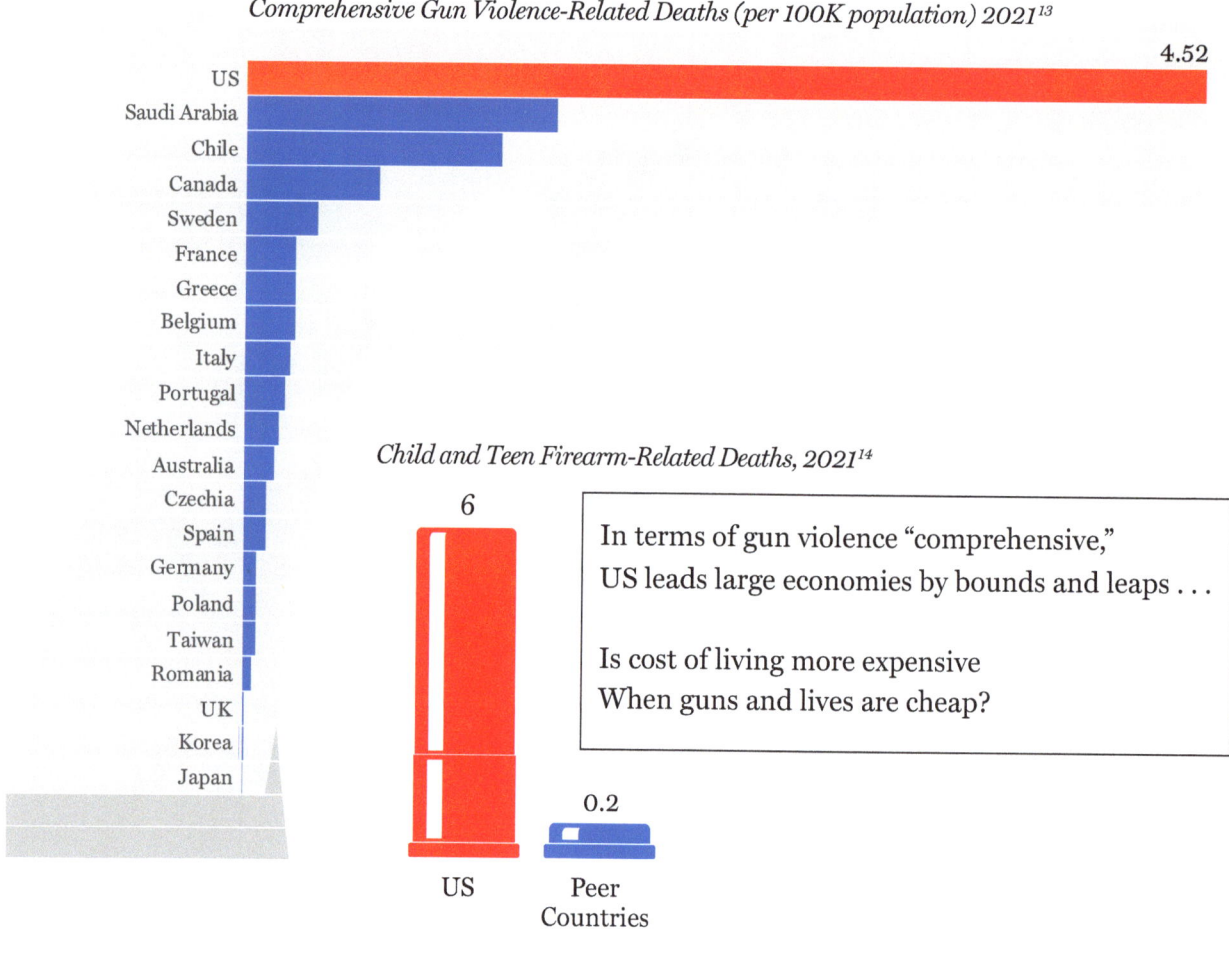

Comprehensive Gun Violence-Related Deaths (per 100K population) 2021[13]

US — 4.52
Saudi Arabia
Chile
Canada
Sweden
France
Greece
Belgium
Italy
Portugal
Netherlands
Australia
Czechia
Spain
Germany
Poland
Taiwan
Romania
UK
Korea
Japan

Child and Teen Firearm-Related Deaths, 2021[14]

6 — US
0.2 — Peer Countries

In terms of gun violence "comprehensive,"
US leads large economies by bounds and leaps . . .

Is cost of living more expensive
When guns and lives are cheap?

[13] "Incidents of firearm mortality per 100K population for high income global economies with populations over 10M," Institute for Health Metrics Evaluation, *United Nations*. Graphics treatment by Ingo Muschenetz.

[14] M. McGough, K. Amin, N. Panchal, C. Cox, "Child and Teen Firearm Mortality in the U.S. and Peer Countries," per 100K population, *KFF.org*, July, 2023; *CDC*. Detailed citation in appendix.

Warning / Surprise — the **exclamation point** *is* meant for conveying strong emotions, HARK! It is overused by the millennials' emphatic insistence to emoji Everything! 👍 ❤️ 🙄 by the Gen-Z'ers, **who** "really mean it!" are over-sensitive, triggered constantly in-active shooter drills, told to:

1. RUN 2. HIDE 3. FIGHT

Pay attention, Jan!

Dan! Eddie! Mia!

this could

save

your life. This is all we've got, all that stands between you and the end of the sentence. **RUN!** (for office)

THE SURFING MADONNA

"The Surfing Madonna" is a 10'x10' mosaic of the "Virgen de Guadalupe" on a surfboard, covertly installed by artist Mark Patterson in Encinitas, CA. It inspired a nonprofit, raising ~$600,000 for humanitarian programs since 2013.

—*Wikipedia.org*

Never once have I crossed myself

I want to believe that—

Mercy, no matter our insecurities

Faith, no matter our flaws

Hope, for a better world

Love, for our neighbors, for our whole selves . . .

You see, *everyday* miracles

(outside of Churches and Temples)

—*we too can walk on water,*

with the right wave beneath us.

Fig. 2 (Save the Ocean)

FOR MALALA, GRETA, AMANDA, MARLEY, MELATI, ISABEL . . .[15]

Just like in any decent Young Adult

story that has / has not yet been

adapted for film (*Hunger Games, Divergent, Sabriel, A Wrinkle in Time,* etc.)

it is up to a teenage girl to save our world—against all odds

while the rest of us are too busy

- pointing out: "It will never work!"
- pointing fingers

at each other

[15] Malala Yousafzai is a Pakistani female education activist who received the 2014 Nobel Peace Prize at 17 years of age. Greta Thunberg is a Swedish environmental activist who inspired a youth movement and was invited to speak to the UN at 16. Amanda Gorman, an American poet and activist, became the first US Youth Poet Laureate at 19. Marley Dias, a US teen, started #100blackgirlbooks to elevate stories featuring women of color. *Forbes* and *TIME* honored her impact by including her in their list of top 30 under 30 and 25 influential teens in 2018. Melati and Isabel Wijsen, Indonesian sisters, were 10 and 12 when they began "Bye Bye Plastic Bags," a nonprofit that led to the ban of plastic bags in Bali and has 60+ locations worldwide. Sources: *Wikipedia, TIME Magazine, Forbes.*

FAMILY DINNER (TALKING POINTS)

You sit down and half the country is everyone's
Crazy Uncle, you know the kind—keeps raving
about *Alien Abductions! Those Damn* _____
(*Liberals / Republicans / Gays / Jesus Freaks / Jews / Gun-Totin'-Idiots / Immigrants /*
Corporations / Hippies / Prohibitionists / Yankees / Federalists / Witches . . .)!
History, that Old Grandmother, keeps looping
her yarn, knitting quietly in her corner chair . . .

Somebody (Mom? Dad? You?) is awkwardly trying to keep the peace:
When was the last time all of us were together like this?
Shoveling food into Uncle's mouth,
hoping he won't do anything . . . irretrievable
and most of us have
too much   of the wrong thing   to eat.

Eventually, a cousin (the "Sweet One") remembers Grandma,
brings her a plate of something soft and easily digestible.
Gams alone seems sustained by all that has come before,
half-deaf and blind to *all the fuss* of current events, and future ones.
Even Death has lost that thrilling excitement—
having come calling so often, he used up all his interesting stories.
Now, everything is a reboot.

Some teenager's parent is one snipe(r) away from fantastically losing it:
How many times do I have to say, "There is no God, but All . . . of us share ONE!"?
What part of "Love Thy Neighbor as Thyself" means punching your brother in the stomach?!

Cousin Mike (aka "Walden 2.0") isn't even here, off watching
survivalist YouTube videos about living off the land
like our illiterate Great-Grandfather from that Ukrainian Shtetl
    . . . *Does anyone miss Borscht, really?*

We are all so desperate for a taste of anything real.

Us Poets keep trying on languages for (bite) size,
ospreys for tongues, diving after silver-scaled words:
Look- STARS! RIVER! TREE! ROCK!
See- *this world, this* LIFE- *Oh!*
the agonizing heart! Oh!

the absolute   aching   beauty of it.

PINK NOISE

[Pink noise, or $1/f$ noise, is a signal . . . with a frequency spectrum (f) . . . discovered in the statistical fluctuations of an extraordinary number of physical and biological systems, including tide and river heights, quasar light emissions, heartbeat, firings of neurons, financial systems.]

—Wikipedia.org

Did you know that the infinitesimal caress that layers
nacre into pearls, conforms to the same pattern as the ocean's steady breath?
Each in-and-out, of each wave, upon the shore—seemingly random,
in fact, keeps to the same rhythms as the human heart and that
($1/f$) procession, which governs (or unites?) such disparate things (!)
as synapses that fire in your brain and, equally complex, financial systems
that, at times, graze calmly and, at times, are Nervous Nellies,
the buzzing of a dying star *and* the sporadic dance of summer raindrops—
is called "Pink Noise."

Oh, Science!
How you pretend to not be poetry, yet
speak in silent prayers.

FAILURE TO THRIVE, A POINT OF INFLECTION

Dr. Harlow's famous "Monkey Love" experiments[16] showed
that baby monkeys choose a soft, warm doll
over the harpy that delivers food
(only two mother archetypes allowed)

It was the 50s, he was a man and wore a lab coat
—permission granted by the "science"
minded for womenfolk to love
their children, hold them even, the tribalistic way
that ancient cultures tend a "savage"
(the best adjective I know for motherhood and social norms)

We have made progress in "Women Studies" since
—it is a field all its own
where her/history gets buried and repeated

[16] "The famous experiments that psychologist Harry Harlow conducted in the 1950s on maternal deprivation in rhesus monkeys were landmarks not only in primatology, but in the evolving science of attachment and loss." The Adoption History Project Webpage, *University of Oregon*, 2024: https://pages. uoregon.edu/adoption/studies/HarlowMLE.htm

#ME TOO, A POINT OF CONSENSUS[17]

1 in every 4 American women and
1 in every 26 American men
experience rape*

Even the "Good" ones,
Even the "Republican" ones,
Even the "Liberal" ones,
Especially, the young ones

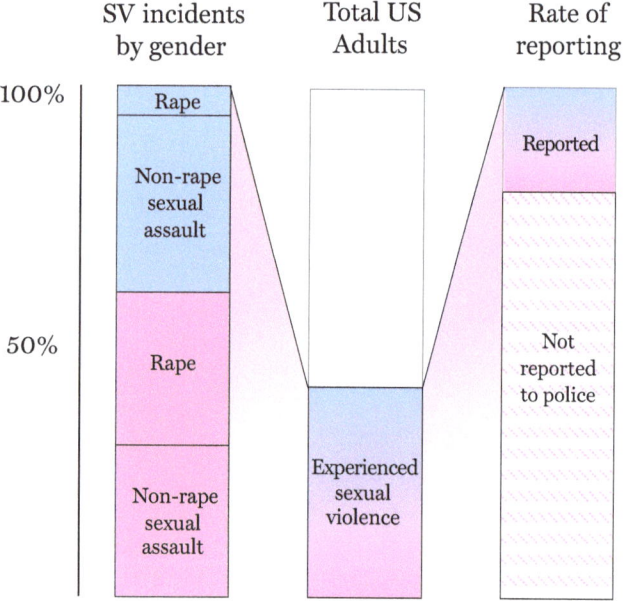

Sexual Violence (SV) in the US, 2022

☐ Women ☐ Men

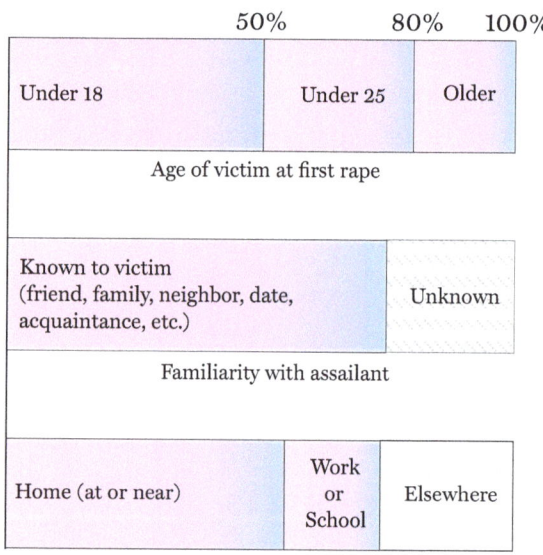

Reported Incidents of Rape in the US, 2020

[17] "Experience rape" refers to incidents of attempted and completed rape, as described in "Preventing Sexual Violence," Fast Facts, *CDC*, 2023. Add'l sources: "Criminal Victimization Report," US Dept. of Justice, Bureau of Justice Statistics, 2022; "Scope of the Problem," *RAINN.org*, Statistics 2020; Criminal Victimization Report, *US Bureau of Justice Statistics*, 2022; US Census; C. Peterson, S. DeGue, C. Florence, C.N. Lokey. "Lifetime Economic Burden of Rape Among US Adults," *Am. Journal of Preventative Medicine*, 2017; "Preventing Sexual Violence," Fast Facts, *CDC*, 2023; "Sexual Violence Prevention Resource for Action Report", CDC, 2016. Detailed citation in appendix.

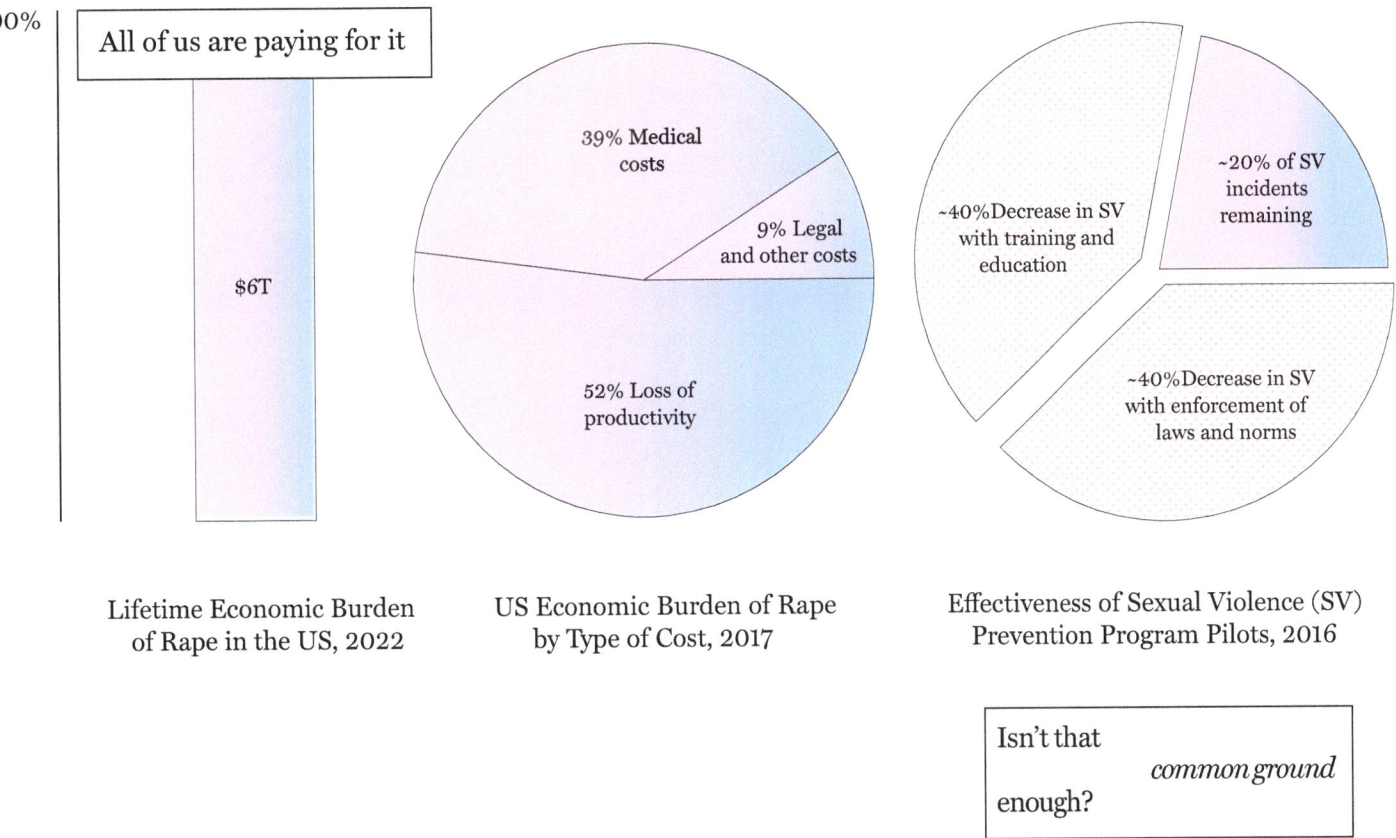

.00%

All of us are paying for it

$6T

39% Medical costs

9% Legal and other costs

52% Loss of productivity

~40%Decrease in SV with training and education

~20% of SV incidents remaining

~40%Decrease in SV with enforcement of laws and norms

Lifetime Economic Burden of Rape in the US, 2022

US Economic Burden of Rape by Type of Cost, 2017

Effectiveness of Sexual Violence (SV) Prevention Program Pilots, 2016

Isn't that *common ground* enough?

I ENROLL MY 11YR-OLD DAUGHTER IN SELF-DEFENSE CLASS

because we all know the statistics

because we've all read the headlines, the stories

we tell ourselves

because, of course,

we all want our children to be safe.

We love our children

because they are our children,

and we love this world

because this is the world we're living in.

Because this is the world we're living in,

I enroll my 11yr-old daughter in Self Defense Class.

SAFETY POINTS, OR 'TIPS FOR WOMEN STAYING SAFE'

Transcribed from the Desoto County Sheriff's Office website[18]

For many, the actions listed below are small-scale habits practiced **on a daily basis**. They are not a guarantee of safety, but are a first line of suggested awareness techniques. Be Alert! Scan the area as you walk. Be aware of your surroundings and walk with confidence. Avoid shopping alone. Try to shop with a friend or relative. Know your surroundings. Keep an eye on the people in front of you as well as behind you. **Carry** your purse close to **your body** and **do not leave it unattended**. Try not to carry too many packages. Place all packages out of sight in your vehicle, preferably in the trunk. Park your vehicle in a well-lighted area. Even in daylight hours, you may want to park near a light pole so if you leave when it is darker, your car will be in a well-lit location. Approach your vehicle with your keys already in your hand. Keep your vehicle doors locked and your windows shut. Look around, under and in your car, especially the back seat, before you get in. When leaving a business **late at night**, (if available) ask a security guard to walk you to your car. Do not go up to just any security guard. Go directly to the kiosk and ask for them to assign an officer to escort you. Predators sometimes dress up to resemble security or other authority figures. When a business requests you to confirm your home address, **whisper** it to them. Broadcasting your home address among strangers in the line could compromise your safety. When checking into a hotel room, if the person at the front desk says your room number out loud, ask them to give you a new room and write the number on a piece of paper. Or when you check-in, ask up front to not say your room number out loud. Your room number should be your business only. Before entering your hotel room, make sure no one is lingering in the hallway. Always immediately lock your hotel room door after you enter. If you call for room service, and you get a knock on your door, do not immediately open the door. Ask: "Who is it?" Make the person on the other side of the door tell you who they are before you open it. If in **doubt** do not open the door and call the front desk. When asking for directions and someone offers to show you the way by having you follow them, do not go. Just ask for them to point you in the right direction. Often, predators want to lure you to a place less crowded where your calls for help can't be heard. Always pour your own drink at a party and bring it with you everywhere...even to the bathroom. This will make it more difficult for someone to drug you via your drink. If you choose to partake in drinking alcohol, remember to have a designated driver. Watch the bartender as he or she pours your drink. To be extra safe, drink wine instead of a cocktail. Mixed drinks take longer to make. You could be easily distracted and miss the bartender (who could be working with a predator) or someone else placing something in your drink. When going out with your friends, decide beforehand you will stick together. Do not let your friend go off alone with any person. Don't check-in on social media apps when you arrive somewhere. Instead, check in as you leave. This way no one will be able to digitally stalk you and know your every move or when you're not at home. Along the same lines, **avoid** tweeting or Facebooking from vacation, especially if your account is public, as it is a way of **letting the world know** your home is unoccupied. When you move into a new residence, check areas for possible hidden cameras. Your landlord, previous tenant or previous owner could be spying on you. **Take Self-Defense** Training. Unfortunately, **no matter how diligently we practice** awareness and **avoidance** techniques, **we** may **find ourselves** in a physical confrontation. If available, it is suggested to take self-defense training. Other considerations for self-defense are l**awful** carrying and possession of self-defense devices.

---

[18] The above advice is taken directly from the Desoto County Sheriff's Office website in 2023. https://www.desotosheriff.com/community/tips_for_women_on_staying_safe!.php.; The image signifies gender inclusivity and can also represent transgender, combining male and female symbols.

WHEN? ALWAYS.

A found poem from the Desoto County Sheriff's Office website [19]

...*Your safety... your hotel... your landlord... your account... your door... your surroundings...*

Your safety... your business... your number... your drink... your friend...

Your purse... your body... your vehicle... your car... your room... your home.

On a daily basis
Carry your body
Do not leave it unattended
Late at night, whisper doubt
Avoid letting the world know
(Take Self-Defense)
No matter how diligently
We practice avoidance
We find ourselves
A w f u l

.... *When?* .... *When?* .... *When?* .... *Always* .... *Always* ....

GENDER NEUTRAL

They're studying the effects of gendering on language[19]
and cultural norms,
how the moon is *feminine* in Spanish and Russian (*Luna*)
but *masculine* in German (*Mond*)
how this alters
our perception of its qualifications—
whether we believe it to be
beautiful, changeable (*f*) or
stoic, abrupt (*m*)—
over 1000 Google links discuss at length

The moon is the moon.

Some promote doing away with sex, but I
(having learned gender from my Mother Tongue
and feeling its lack like a missing limb when I try bending English)
am fascinated, mouth-hungry
to embrace each understanding of our world,
uncomfortable and broken as it is
learning to speak again and again.
There is something revealing about seeing the moon
through every lexiconic, scientific, and artistic notion
and still not having enough
words to fill the sky

[19] S. Briggs, "Do gender fair languages affect gender equality? Here's the research," *Berlitz*, July 2022, https://www.berlitz.com/blog/does-language-affect-gender-equality

THE EARTH REMEMBERS HER TEENAGE YEARS

How many times she almost destroyed herself.
How she was nothing but molten, constantly flaring, combustible—
how she just kept *erupting*
under the weight of her own gravity.

How alone she felt
in what she thought was the darkness
between herself and the galaxy that birthed her,
without even the moon yet for company.

How she beckoned every rock hurtling through space
to make a home of her.
How she cratered, even as she became more solid
and cooled . . . eventually.

How slow it all felt then, those millennia
which now seem only an instant, looking back
in awe of herself, of that unquenchable fire
still buried deep in her core.

How she watches us, the life she brought forth
despite *everything*.
How she forgives our own endless thrashing.
How she wishes (knowing already) it could be easier.

INSPIRATION POINT

In this version of history, Marge

never went to college / Marge went to college briefly / Marge went to

an all-girls college in the Roaring 1920's / in pre-revolution Iran / in 2022 Afghanistan / in 2005 Harvard,

when the school's President attributed underrepresentation of women in science to:

> "... different availability of aptitude at the high end ... a level of commitment
>
> that a much higher fraction of married men have been historically prepared to make
>
> than of married women."[20]

Controversy arose

when Marge wore pants / rode a bike / drove a car / played baseball / practiced medicine.

Marge was jailed / sent to an asylum for reading too much and managing her own finances.

Marge was rich and White / Marge was poor and White / Marge was rich and Latina /

Latina and gay / Black / Indigenous / Jewish / Muslim ...

Marge went to a Catholic boarding school / a convent / a convention /

the 1977 National Women's Conference—she participated!

in the women councils that governed ancient civilizations alongside the men.

Marge studied art and mothering, gave birth

to Astrophysics, Jesus, and Software Engineering[21] /

walked alone late at night through the city center /

the college campus / the grocery store parking lot / the corn field /

the timeline

> *(Oh, the magnificent view!)*

Fearless.

---

[20] "Harvard President Summers' Remarks About Women in Science, Engineering," *PBS News Radio Hour*, 2005

[21] Mary Sommerville, the first "scientist'"(as opposed to "man of science") combined the fields of astronomy, mathematics, and physical forces in her 1831 translation and expansion of Lapace's *Mécanique Céleste*; In *The Bible*, Virgin Mary birthed Jesus; Ada Lovelace (1815-52) is widely acknowledged as the first computer programmer, while the first US software engineers during the early 1900's were all women. Sources include *Wikipedia.org*.

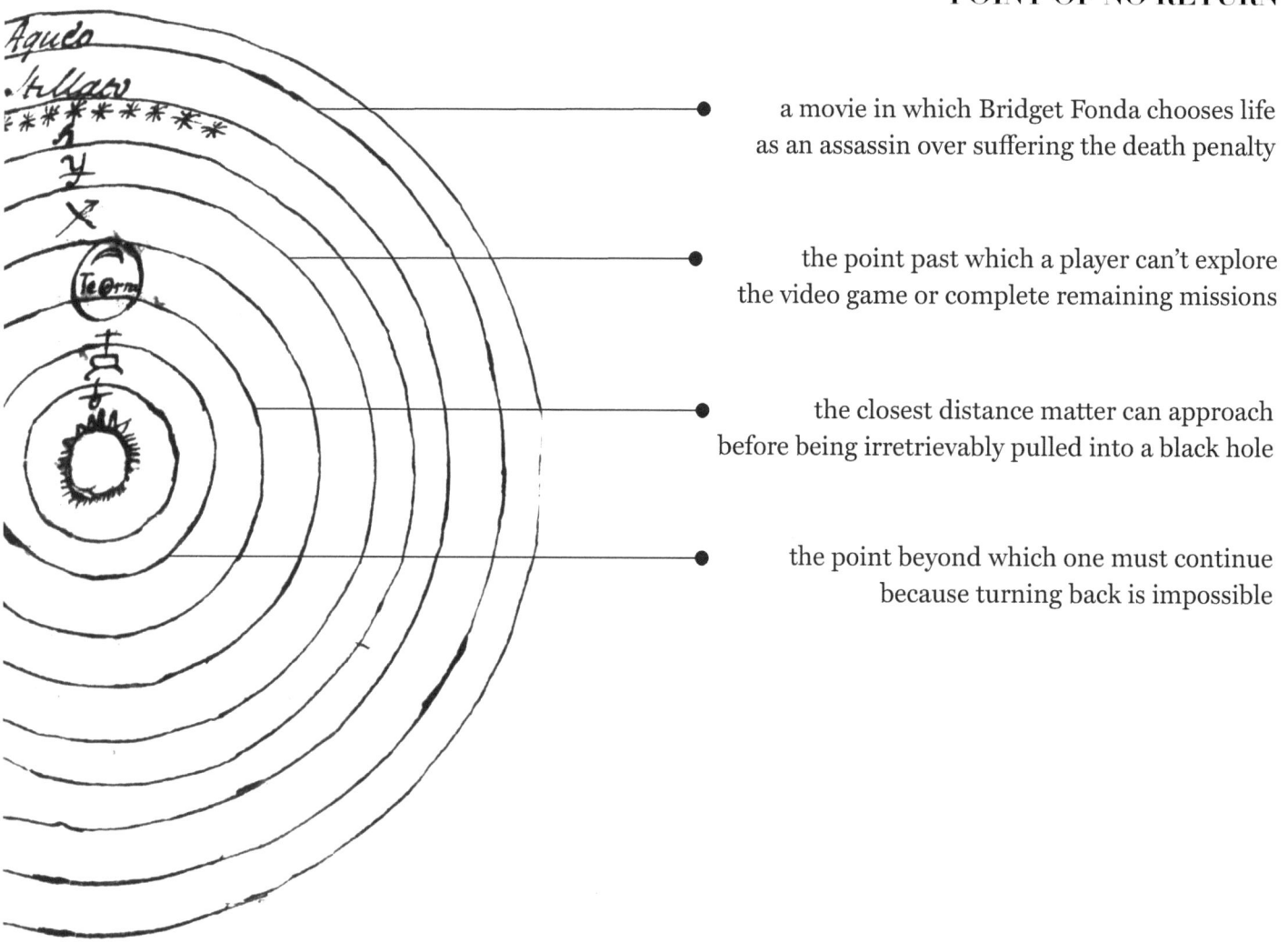

a movie in which Bridget Fonda chooses life
as an assassin over suffering the death penalty

the point past which a player can't explore
the video game or complete remaining missions

the closest distance matter can approach
before being irretrievably pulled into a black hole

the point beyond which one must continue
because turning back is impossible

STOP THIS POEM!

Unpin your thoughts—it's not only possible, it's been done before
and more than just once or twice, by people just as imperfect
as we are, with even less opportunity to get it right . . .

Listen, we are not the first nor the last to stand here
arguing, to sit here crying, etc . . .

Stop this poem!
Exit the room.
Go—

        look at the birds in the garden instead—read
          the leaves while they're still on the tree.

        Ripen to fullness. Become *un-pluckable*
          —tend this feathering/yearning . . .

        Ask the sun how to meadow,
          then, ask your fingers.

        Be long in this world.

NOTES

This collection stands on contributions of trailblazers in the study of gender dynamics and of countless unsung heroes whose brilliance remains hidden by prejudice and custom. An endless thank you to all those who paved the way, including Hayley Mitchell Haugen and Sheila-Na-Gig Editions. Your trust in my vision and kind support of risk-taking writers made the process of bringing this book into the world with you a joy.

A huge, HUGE! shout-out to my husband and love of my life, Ingo, whose beautiful graphic design, layout, and typography skills are evident in the cover and throughout this book. Thank you for sharing your incredible heart and talent with me. Emmet and Eloise, my kids (and literal "skin in the game"), thank you for inspiring me everyday to work for a better future. I love you.

Heartfelt thanks as well to the generous and gifted writers who endorsed this collection. I am honored and lucky to know you. Special hug/heart/yay! emoji to Katie Manning, who rooted for this project from early days and whose friendship is one of the blessings of my writerly life. I am deeply grateful for my family, friends, and all the women, men, and children in my life who are sources of innumerable "every day miracles"—love, perseverance, wisdom, empathy, and strength.

Dear Reader, thank you for spending time with my work. I hope it resonated with you.

Wherever possible, I tried to use the most reliable publicly available data sources for my poems. I am not a professional scientist or sociologist, and, at times, it was frustrating not having access to more comprehensive data sets. (Apologies for any inadvertent oversights on my part.) The very fact that some of the most "recent" available data on these issues is over 10 years old (as in #ME TOO) is telling. Nevertheless, I am sharing the facts and figures as I found them.

The links and detailed sources supporting the data poems in this collection are listed on the next page and linked via QR Code. I hope you engage with the information and the topics they cover, interrogate their meaning, and draw your own conclusions about what they tell you.

DETAILED CITATIONS

100% Mom

CDC, https://www.cdc.gov/nchs/fastats/womens-health.htm , https://www.cdc.gov/hearher/pregnancy-related-deaths/index.html; *Common Wealth Fund*, https://www.commonwealthfund.org/blog/2022/us-maternal-mortality-crisis-continues-worsen-international-comparison; "The World's Women 2020 Trends and Statistics," *United Nations* https://www.un.org/en/desa/world's-women-2020; *Oxfam International Inequality Reports*: 2020, 2021, "Hard Work is not Enough: Women in Low-Paid Jobs," *National Women's Law Center*, July 2023, https://nwlc.org/resource/when-hard-work-is-not-enough-women-in-low-paid-jobs/

Low Point

"The SPM child poverty rate more than doubled, from 5.2 to 12.4 percent from 2021 to 2022," Supplemental Poverty Measures 2017-2022, *US Census*, https://www.census.gov/newsroom/stories/poverty-awareness-month.html; "The Expanded Child Tax Credit Briefly Slashed Child Poverty," *NPR.org*, 2022, https://www.npr.org/2022/01/27/1075299510/the-expanded-child-tax-credit-briefly-slashed-child-poverty-heres-what-else-it-d; "The Expanded Child Tax Credit Is Gone. The Battle Over It Remains," *NY Times*, 2022, https://www.nytimes.com/2022/11/25/us/politics/child-tax-credit.html (Congress approved $1.7T in 2022 discretionary spending. The pandemic child tax credit expansion cost was ~$100B per year.)

Point Blank

"Comprehensive Gun Violence-Related Deaths" includes all incidents of firearm mortality, accidental and intentional, per 100K population for high income global economies with populations over 10 million. Source: Institute for Health Metrics Evaluation, *United Nations* https://www.healthdata.org/news-events/insights-blog/acting-data/gun-violence-united-states-outlier; Data Sources: *CDC*; M.McGough, K. Amin, N. Panchal, C. Cox, "Child and Teen Firearm Mortality in the U.S. and Peer Countries," *KFF.org*, Jul, 2023; https://www.kff.org/mental-health/issue-brief/child-and-teen-firearm-mortality-in-the-u-s-and-peer-countries/

#ME TOO

Criminal Victimization Report, *US Dept. of Justice, Bureau of Justice Statistics*, 2022 https://bjs.ojp.gov/document/cv22.pdf; *US Census* population count, https://www.census.gov/quickfacts/fact/table/US/PST045222; "Lifetime Economic Burden of Rape Among US Adults," *Am. Journal of Preventative Medicine*, 2017 https://www.ajpmonline.org/article/S0749-3797(16)30615-8/fulltext, Estimated economic cost applied the CDC 2014 lifetime cost of $122.5K per victim to all rape victims (adult and minor) based on 2022 estimates from Dept. of Justice. "Preventing Sexual Violence," Fast Facts, *CDC*, 2023; Pilot program effectiveness sourced from the "Sexual Violence Prevention Resource for Action Report," *CDC*, 2016, https://www.cdc.gov/violenceprevention/pdf/SV-Prevention-Resource_508.pdf https://www.cdc.gov/violenceprevention/sexualviolence/fastfact.html

REFERENCES

Additional sources that helped inspire and inform this project:

Lisa Damour, *Untangled: Guiding Teenage Girls Through the Seven Transitions Into Adulthood*, Ballantine Books, 2017

Lilian Faderman, *Woman: The American History of an Idea*, Yale University Press, 2022

Sandra M. Gilbert and Susan Gubar, *Still Mad: American Women Writers and the Feminist Imagination*, W.W. Norton & Company, 2021

Anna Leahy, *What Happened Was*, Small Harbor Publishing, 2021

Mary Pipher and Sara Pipher Gilliam, *Reviving Ophelia 25th Anniversary Edition: Saving the Selves of Adolescent Girls*, Riverhead Books, 2019

Jessy Randall, *Mathematics for Ladies, Poems on Women in Science*, Goldsmith's Press, 2022

Krista Tippett, *On Being* podcast

Pádraig Ó Tuama, *Poetry Unbound* podcast and *In the Shelter: Finding a home in the world*, Hodder & Stoughton, 2015

ABOUT THE AUTHOR

MIT alumna and former Bain & Co. management consultant, Jane Yevgenia Muschenetz arrived in the US as a Jewish child refugee from Soviet Ukraine. She earned her BA in Political Science from UCSD, her MBA from the MIT Sloan School of Business, and learned (via extensive on-the-job-training) to mother two "mostly American" kids—never once considering how much this education would aid her in the writing of poetry.

Recognized in 2023 by San Diego County for excellence in poetry performance, Jane has appeared on KPBS Midday Edition and in numerous publications. Her debut chapbook, *All the Bad Girls Wear Russian Accents* (Kelsay Books, 2023), won the 2024 California Press Women Communications Prize in Creative Verse and the 2024 San Diego Writers Festival Short Poetry Collection of the Year. An emerging writer and artist, Jane's additional honors include multiple Best of the Net and Pushcart Prize nominations and *The Good Life Review* Honeybee Poetry Prize (2022). Connect with Jane and more of her work at www.PalmFrondZoo.com

COLOPHON

This book was typeset in Miller Text, which draws inspiration from typefaces crafted in Scotland in the early 1800s. Popularized as Scotch Roman typefaces, used extensively in newspapers, their design, including vertical stress, roundness, and notably tall x-heights, offer an energizing effect and excellent readability at small sizes. The Miller version used here is via Adobe, designed by Matthew Carter of Carter & Cone type foundry.

The titles of the poems and the title of this book are set in Didot, a typeface named after the French Didot family of printers. The neoclassical font is evocative of the Age of Enlightenment, a.k.a. the Age of Reason. 1700s and 1800s Europe is noted for embracing the scientific method as a guiding principle in philosophy, art, and theology. Didot was popularly used alongside the CBS television network's "eye" logo.

Miller Text and Didot in combination are reminiscent of font families used within the magazine, *Scientific American*. Since 1845, *Scientific American* has played a key role in democratizing science, making complex scientific ideas accessible and engaging to a broad audience.

The art that Ingo and Jane Muschenetz created for this book is influenced by scientific illustrations from 1600's-2000's, media infographics, and protest art. Several of them expand or manipulate licensed stock images. The cover collage includes clippings from their home town's paper, *The San Diego Union Tribune*.

Sheila-Na-Gig Editions

www.ingramcontent.com/pod-product-compliance
Lightning Source LLC
Chambersburg PA
CBHW041434120626
46547CB00002B/215